For Wilhelmina

PETER ZUMTHOR
2002–2007

Buildings and Projects

Volume 4

Edited by Thomas Durisch

Scheidegger & Spiess

Volume 1   1985–1989

What I Do

Atelier Zumthor, Haldenstein, Graubünden
Shelter for Roman Archaeological Ruins, Chur, Graubünden
Caplutta Sogn Benedetg, Sumvitg, Graubünden
Spittelhof Housing Complex, Biel-Benken near Basel
Rindermarkt Apartment Building, Zurich
Rothorn Gondola Station, Valbella, Graubünden
Apartments for Senior Citizens, Masans, Chur, Graubünden
Bregenz Art Museum, Austria

Volume 2   1990–1997

Gugalun House, Versam, Graubünden
Therme Vals, Graubünden
Topography of Terror, Berlin, Germany
Herz Jesu Church, Munich, Germany
Laban Centre for Movement and Dance, London, England
Swiss Sound Box, Expo 2000, Hanover, Germany
Luzi House, Jenaz, Graubünden
Kolumba Art Museum, Cologne, Germany

Volume 3   1998–2001

Poetic Landscape, Bad Salzuflen, Germany
Zumthor House, Haldenstein, Graubünden
Mountain Hotel, Tschlin, Graubünden
I Ching Gallery, Dia Center for the Arts, Beacon, New York, USA
Harjunkulma Apartment Building, Jyväskylä, Finland
Pingus Winery, Valbuena de Duero, Spain
Bruder Klaus Field Chapel, Wachendorf, Germany
Additional Cabins, Pension Briol, Barbian-Dreikirchen, Italy

Volume 4   2002–2007

Galerie Bastian, Berlin, Germany	7
Redevelopment of De Meelfabriek, Leiden, Holland	17
Summer Restaurant Insel Ufnau, Lake Zurich	35
Corporate Learning Center, Aabach Estate, Risch, Zug	51
Almannajuvet Zinc Mine Museum, Sauda, Norway	73
Güterareal Residential Development, Lucerne	91
A Tower for Therme Vals, Graubünden	109
Leis Houses, Oberhus and Unterhus, Vals, Graubünden	121
Hisham's Palace, Jericho, Palestinian Territories	149
Steilneset Memorial, Vardø, Norway	163

Volume 5   2008–2013

Nomads of Atacama Hotel, San Pedro de Atacama, Chile
Bregenzerwald House of Craftsmanship, Andelsbuch, Austria
Chivelstone House, Devon, England
Los Angeles County Museum of Art, LACMA, California, USA
New City Gate with Theater and Café, Isny im Allgäu, Germany
Adaptable Theater for Riom Castle, Riom, Graubünden
House of Seven Gardens, Doha, Qatar
Serpentine Gallery Pavilion, London, England
Perm State Art Gallery, Perm, Russia

List of Works 1968–2013
Texts by Peter Zumthor
Biography
Collaborators 1985–2013
The Work of Many
Acknowledgments
Picture Credits

Galerie Bastian, Berlin, Germany
2002–2003

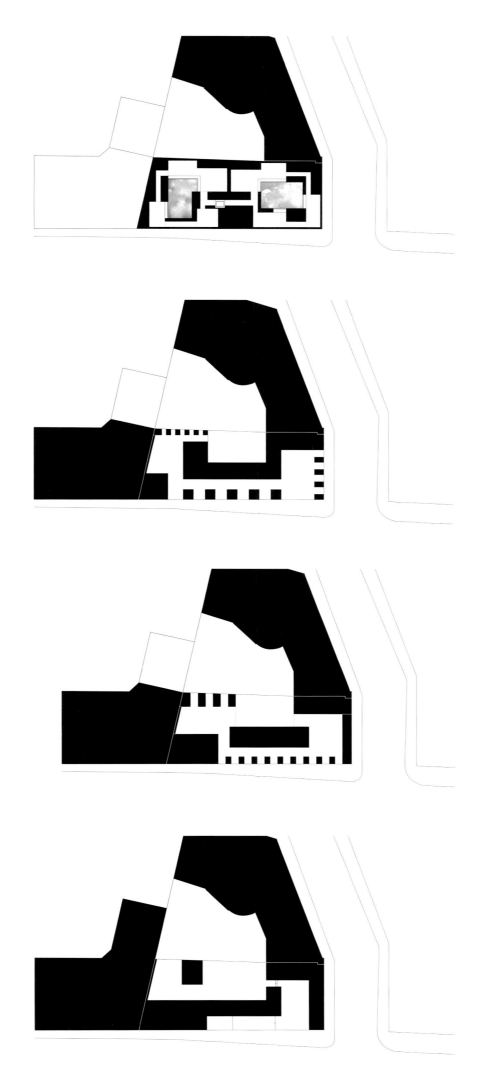

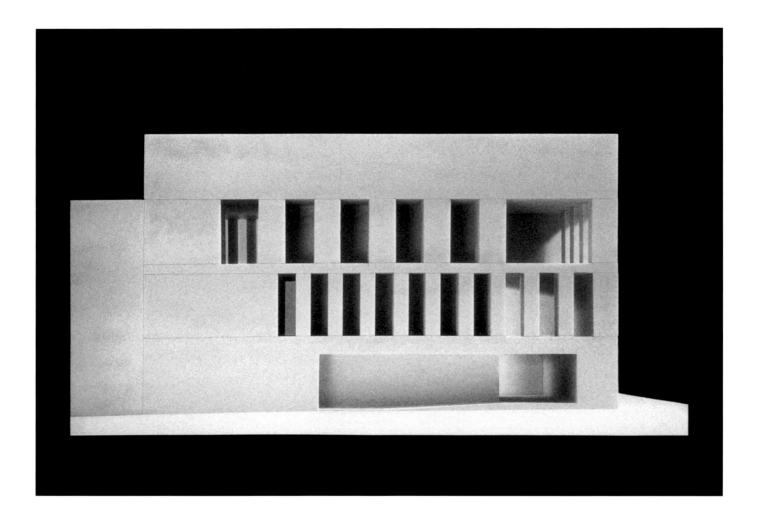

The client, a private art collector, wanted a gallery building with two apartments. It was to be built on an empty corner lot on the Kupfergraben, near the iron footbridge directly across from the Museum Island in Berlin.

The design played with the accumulated power and the cool elegance of Prussian Classicism emanating from the buildings assembled there. The new building's theme was to be large, precisely cut stone blocks. We tried to have the design emphasize the sense of clarity and the serenity of the surroundings. At the beginning, we envisioned a special set of child's building blocks, made of stone. Moving on from there meant elaborating on the building blocks to define their mass, and scale, and to find their rules. The gallery building would be an architectural whole, devised to create and accommodate special spaces.

Where this journey would have led we do not know. What would have become of the white Carrara marble we used for the model—chalk-white concrete?

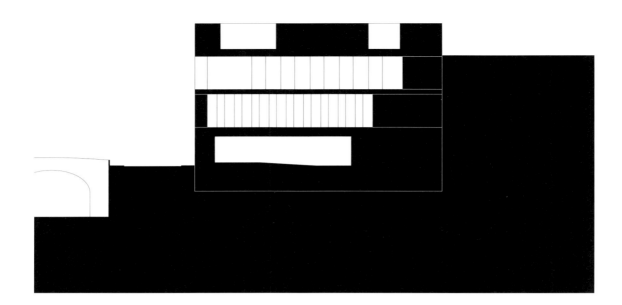
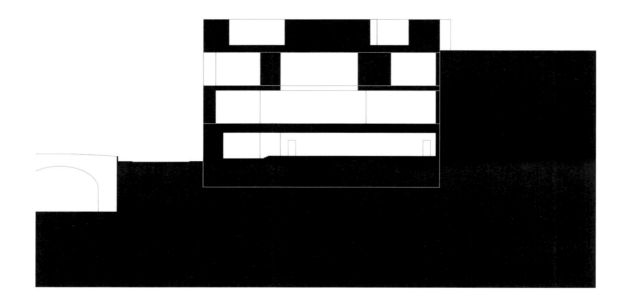

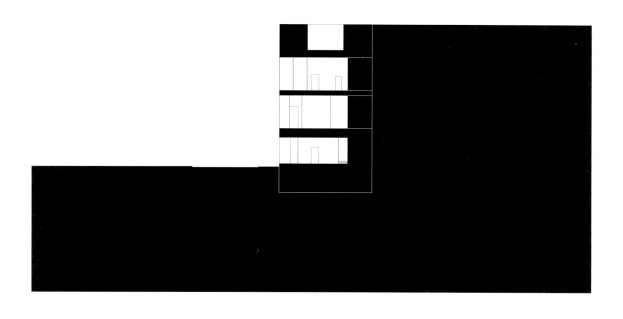
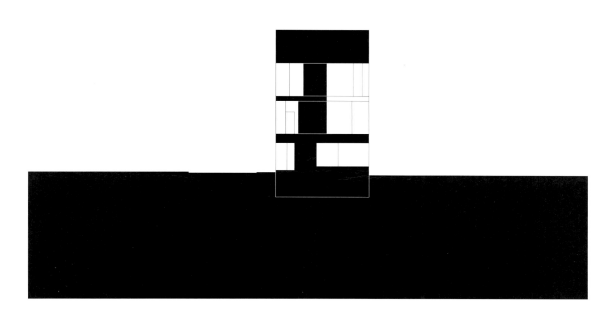
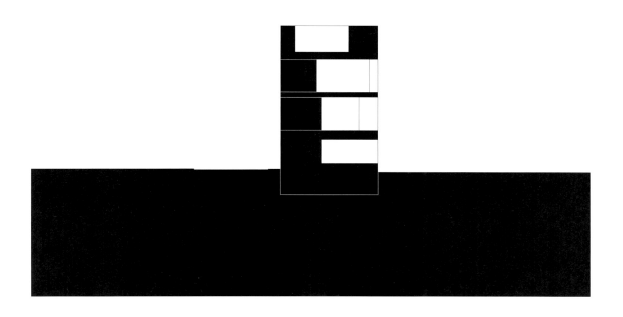

Redevelopment of De Meelfabriek, Leiden, Holland
since 2002

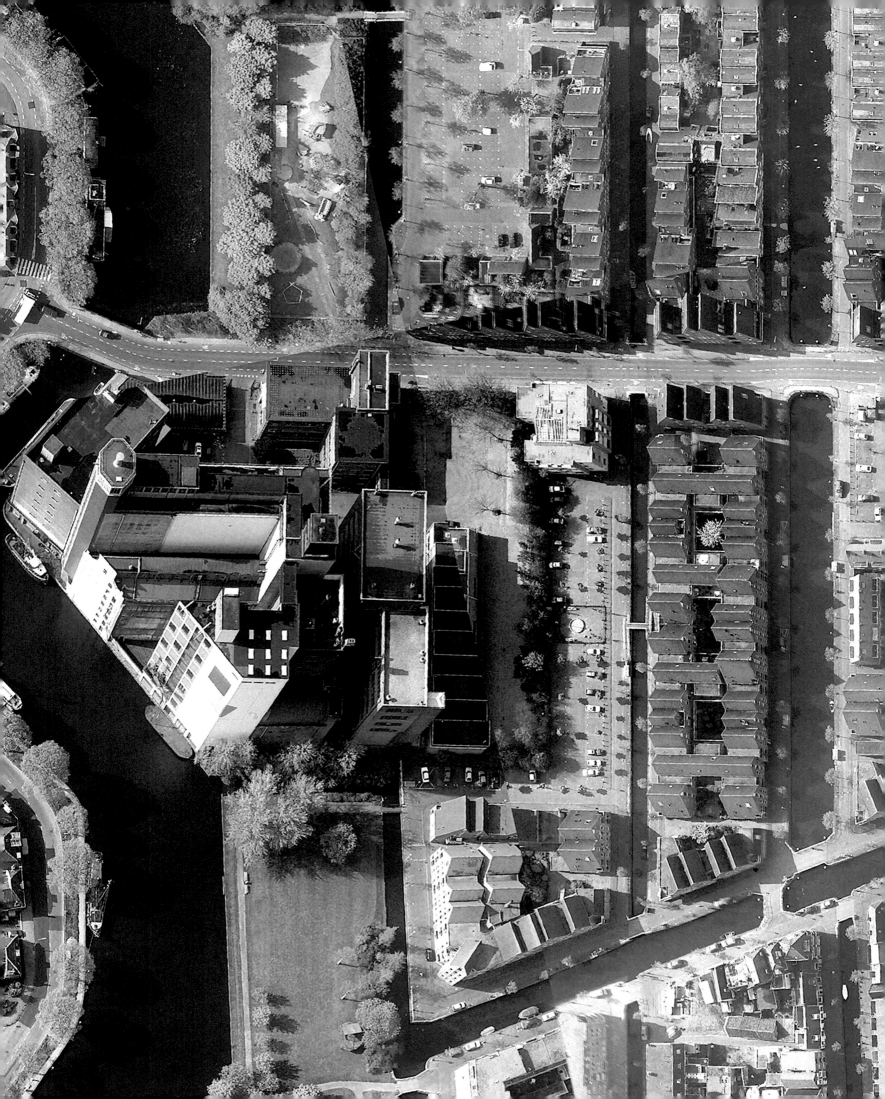

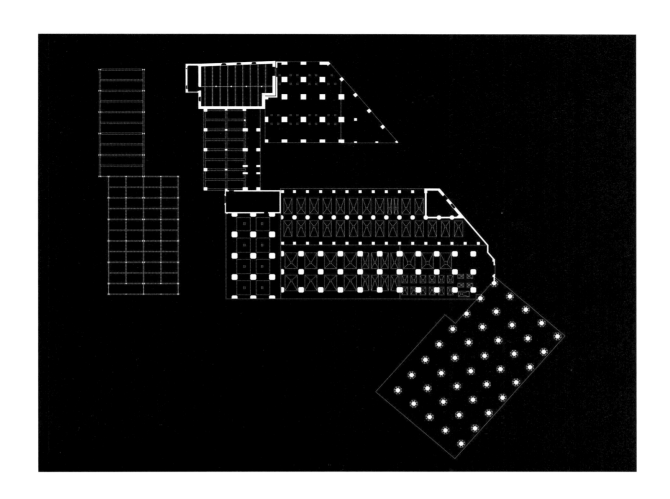
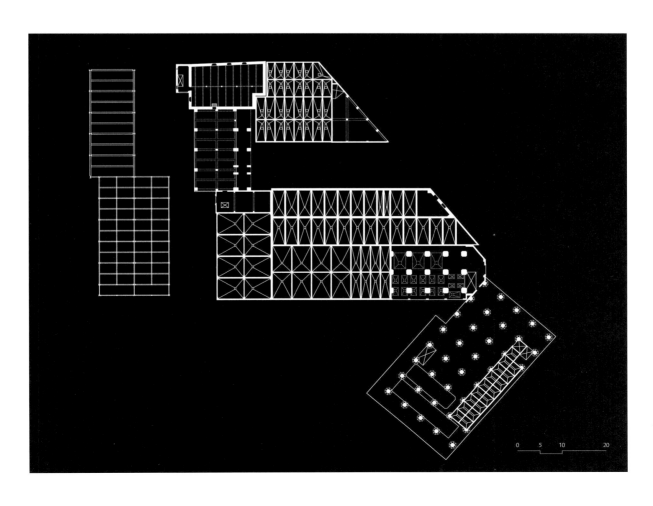

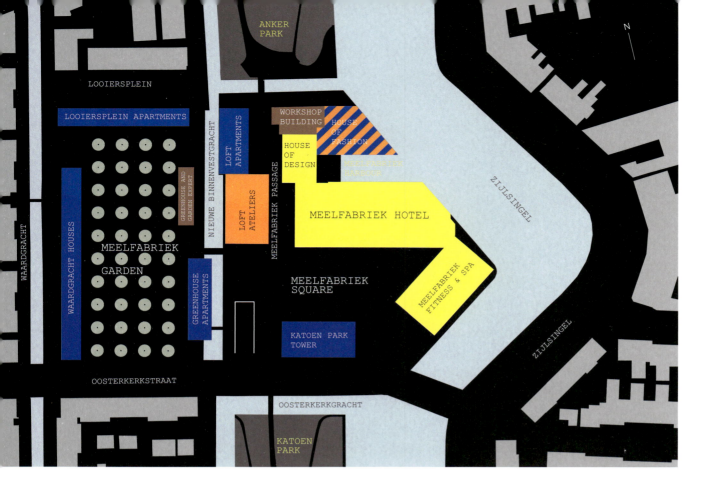

Photographs from the first half of the twentieth century reveal vigorous industrial activity on the northern edge of the Old City of Leiden. They show that the Zijlsingel, originally part of the city fortifications, was used as an industrial canal. On its banks, one can see a cotton spinning mill (*Katoenfabriek*), an anchor factory, and between them a flour mill complex (*Meelfabriek*) with large production and storage facilities, all crowded together on a projecting rampart of the earlier fortifications. The mill has grown with history, constantly undergoing change since it was originally built in 1883. Older buildings were demolished, renovated, or expanded, and new ones added.

Today the Meelfabriek, as it is called in Dutch, seems like a piece of frozen history in Leiden's industrial landscape, for in 1988 the mill ceased operations. It has been empty ever since. Its neighbors, the anchor factory and the cotton mill, have been torn down, making room to restore the green strip that was originally part of the city fortifications. Thus were created two open spaces: the Anchor Park and the Cotton Park.

Building development in the adjoining area of the Old City behind the factories was not as auspicious. The neighborhood contained workers' houses, which have since been demolished and replaced by humdrum row houses. City life has never come back to these new buildings. There are no public spaces in the neighborhood that people would want to visit, and the flour mill, an artifact from earlier times that dominates the entire area, is an impressive monument, but also a forbidding colossus. Now an official industrial heritage site, it stands there imposing, empty, and, until recently, inaccessible.

Given this situation, our first task was to suggest city planning strategies and measures. The part of town surrounding the Meelfabriek was to be reinvigorated. The focus of our work was the old factory complex. It is part of the city's history and identity, and has the potential to assimilate new life. The robust architectural structures of the old factory buildings offer many different possibilities for use. New urban energies could emerge.

We defined our concept of urban renewal in a master plan that was approved by the city of Leiden in 2007. Its basic principle is that the area is to be used both for work and for living; it proposes creating publicly accessible spaces and institutions; and it suggests a comprehensive mix of different uses for the old and new buildings that will allow a vital city center to arise: lofts, family apartments, residences for young and old, ateliers, workshops and commercial spaces for artists and craftsmen, restaurants, cafes, spaces for cultural activities (exhibitions, film, theater, seminars, workshops), and stores for everyday needs. In addition, special services will exert a magnetic attraction throughout the city of Leiden, such as an exclusive hotel or a wellness center offering special benefits to body and soul.

The master plan establishes an architectural dialogue between old and new structures. New buildings will stand in contrast to the old industrial facilities of the mill. The ensemble will be invigorated by the tension between old and new. The original building types will still be visible and will retain their identity. Each new building will have its own form and style, and yet also be incorporated into the composition as a whole. Inspired by the old factory, the new quarter will take shape as a community of distinctive architectural personalities.

The disposition of buildings and open areas will generate new, largely traffic-free public spaces: the Meelfabriek Plaza, the Meelfabriek Park, a pedestrian passage leading all through the former factory site from the Anchor Park to the Cotton Park. Traditional streetscapes will follow the Waardsgracht and the Looiersplein. A canal (*gracht*) that had been filled in will be reconstructed in the middle of the area as an extension of the Binnenoostsingel, with a bridge for pedestrians to connect the Meelfabriek Plaza and the Meelfabriek Park. On the Zijlsingel, by the silos, there will be a small harbor for water taxis. A network of open passages and plazas will link the entrances to the buildings, stores, and restaurants. The Meelfabriek quarter will be integrated into the city.

The architectural power of these historic industrial buildings has been a constant companion and inspiration while working on the planning and renewal of the Meelfabriek quarter over the past ten years. It is fascinating to see how much the support structures vary in type and shape depending on the original use of each building: the mushroom-shaped columns in the flour warehouse, like a forest of increasingly sturdy supports from the upper to the lower floors; the indestructible character of the concrete-frame construction of the Schoonmakerij; the elegant steel skeleton of the Molengebouw and the Riffellokaal; or the dense honeycomb structure of the grain silos. There is something sacred about the colonnades at ground level where they support the weight of the silos with their concrete funnels suspended like stalactites in the rectangles formed by the columns. The concatenation of these building types, designed for heavy loads and special production processes, is impressive.

As usual in industrial architecture, the interiors of the buildings are basically identical with their load-bearing structure, which will be completely preserved in our master plan. Initial studies have demonstrated that new types of use can be retrofitted without problems, while the architectural form and style profit from the basic historical substance of the buildings. Industrial heft as a backdrop for modern life.

However, we do say farewell to the old façades. The single glazing of the windows, the uninsulated exterior walls, and the simple industrial detailing cannot successfully be imported into our era. All the historic buildings will be given a new face, façades that will work with the old structures, shedding new light on them—transparent and elegant.

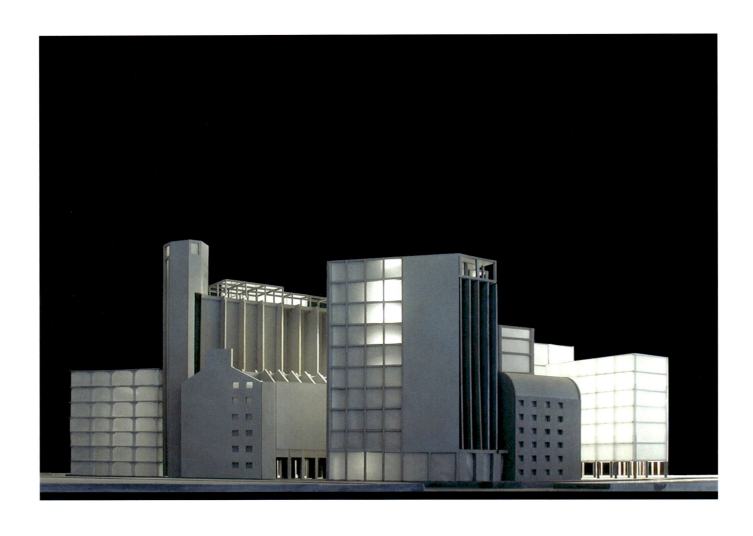

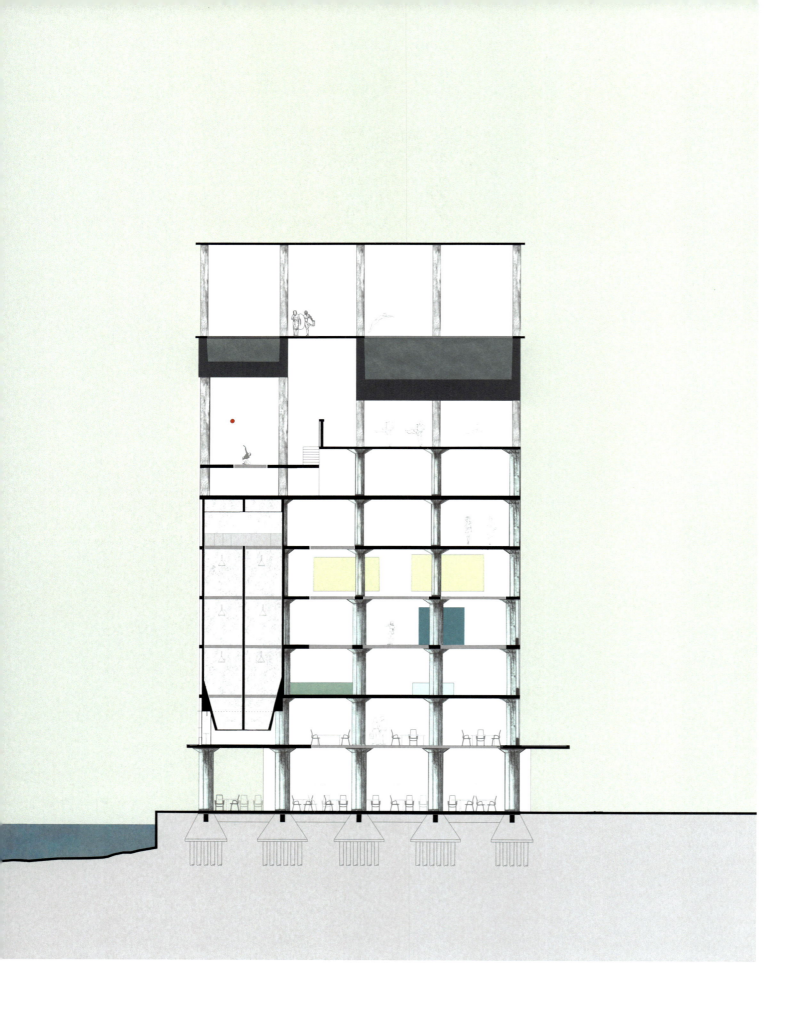

Summer Restaurant, Insel Ufnau, Lake Zurich, Schwyz
2003–2011

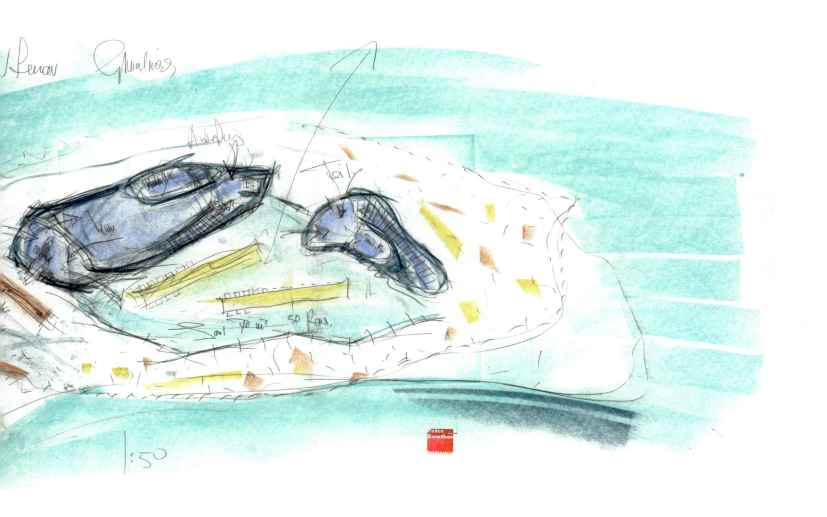

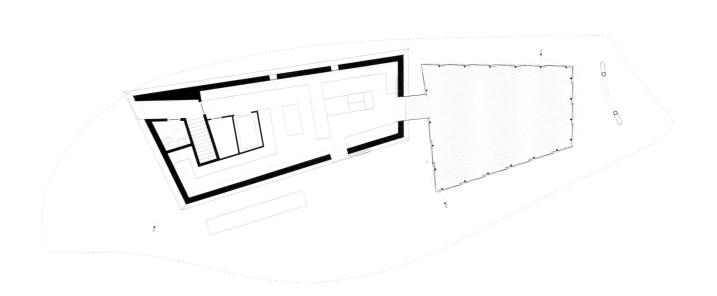

The island of Ufnau in Lake Zurich is a jewel. The two churches, Sts. Peter and Paul and St. Martin from the twelfth century, The Two Ravens inn from the Baroque period, a great barn and the Arnstein, a little pleasure house in the trees in which the monks from the Einsiedeln Monastery once spent their holidays, all blend with the topography and landscape of the island. For over a thousand years the island has belonged to the Einsiedeln Monastery. This enduring relationship to its owner may well explain why the ensemble of the island has been able to preserve an old-style kind of beauty in the midst of the badly overbuilt landscape around Lake Zurich.

The topography of the island, its banks lined with trees, its pastureland, the vineyards, and the thoughtfully placed buildings work together in a harmonious relationship. The island radiates serenity. That is the sweetness Gottfried Keller is talking about when he describes his homeland and the landscape of Lake Zurich. But when I see the island rising up out of the water before me like the flat back of a great fish from the Ice Age glaciers that once covered everything in this area I also see something older, more geological.

Was it presumptuous to share with my client, the Einsiedeln Monastery, the idea of enriching this special place with a new building? From a practical standpoint, there were good reasons to do so. The island is a popular excursion destination in the region. In the summer, the cruise boats on Lake Zurich make stops at the island several times a day. On a nice weekend there are hundreds of people landing there. The outmoded gastronomic facilities cannot keep pace with the demand.

So the Monastery commissioned us to plan a new restaurant for the summer visitors to the island: it would have a small dining room for special occasions, a kitchen, sanitary facilities, and a large open-air restaurant. Visitors would be offered simple but good quality food and drink. Hospitality was our main concern.

Our project features a wooden shell roof held up by delicate supports; it is designed to communicate a sense of shelter and *Schermen*. This Alemannic dialect word commonly used in Switzerland means "refuge" or "cover"; it has remained an important concept for me. Beneath the sheltering arched shell, its shape silhouetting the gentle curves of the island itself, there is a block of masonry looking like a boulder: we called this the Kitchen Stone. It accommodates the kitchen and the service areas. We designed the small dining room as a wooden platform floating just above the ground: this we called the Dance Floor. It is just adjacent to the Kitchen Stone and is encased in glass panels that can be opened or closed depending on wind and weather.

The floating roof of the new restaurant seeks out the topographic midpoint of the island, a crest in its longitudinal axis just faintly discernible beneath the gently undulating carpet of meadows. Here, the restaurant would form part of a small farmstead along with the old barn and The Two Ravens inn. The traditional gravel-covered eating area outdoors, with wooden tables and benches beneath shade trees, unites the new construction with the two older buildings. The gravel-covered area would extend under the new roof shell. Food and drinks could be ordered and picked up in the sheltered area under the roof. On nice summer days, when island traffic is at its peak, the food would be served directly from the large counter.

Our design involved removing the clunky annex of The Two Ravens, which has compromised the harmony of the inn since the late 1930s. This would disappear along with other, more recently built auxiliary structures. The atmosphere of the new, more harmonious ensemble is neater and brighter, enhanced by a touch of festive elegance.

The then abbot Martin Werlen and the monastic community liked our project, and so did the authorities and the majority of the voters in the municipality of Pfäffikon, to which the island belongs politically. But the project also had opponents, and these people went to court. The island of Ufnau lies in a protected zone. We drew up a second design, in which the new construction was brought closer to the existing ensemble. The authorities and the cantonal court in Schwyz, in whose territory the island lies, approved our plan. But in the end, the Swiss Federal Court decided that no new freestanding building could be erected on Ufnau, not even if it were to replace an unlovely addition of fairly recent origin.

Corporate Learning Center, Aabach Estate, Risch, Zug
2003–2013

The Aabach estate is one of the historic villa properties built along the western shore of Lake Zug since the late 1800s. Part of the property is on a beautiful stretch of lakefront. There is an old boathouse and a wooden dock leading out into the lake; reeds grow in the shallow water at the edge, and big willow, alder, and ash trees line the winding path along the bank of the lake. At times you could almost be strolling through an English park. A bit further, meadow pastures lead to a gently rounded hilltop. You can practically feel the grinding glacier that formed it a long time ago. A villa was built there in the late 1920s with a French-style garden. Somehow it does not quite fit into the rest of the landscape, for just in the hollow behind the ridge there are several older stands of elms, hornbeams, yews, and magnolias in the natural English style.

A pharmaceutical company has acquired the estate and wants to build a training center there. Our concept would allocate the various functions of the center to separate and distinct buildings that blend into the landscape. Our intention is to establish a harmony of landscape and architecture, essentially creating a campus nestled in a park.

The network of trails paved with natural materials is for pedestrians only. The paths lead informally from building to building. The different landscape situations are developed with restraint. The experience of place and landscape is heightened. The elements of the park in the English style, including spontaneous growth, are to be preserved and strengthened with new plantings; the building on the hill and its French garden will be removed.

A new patch of landscape will be added to the southern end of the park, which ends at the natural border of the meandering Aabach, where it empties into the lake. We envision restoring the alluvial plain that once bordered the brook up to where it flows into the lake. Five long wooden structures running in the same direction as the brook will be placed in between the vegetation typical of such a flood plain—for the most part newly planted willows and alders, ash trees and maples. Built on stilts, they house the learning center's guest rooms.

All the new constructions of the center are sensitive to the topography and the landscape and are sited with this in mind. The auditorium, restaurant, and studios are grouped around the hilltop. The ridge where the villa stands today will remain open, while the new restaurant extends back into the swale and looks out from the rear over the hilltop and onto the lake. The auditorium is nestled in the swale and the gym reaches out to the trees in the flood plain in front of the hill. Despite their considerable size, all the structures are built exclusively of solid wood. Inside and out. And they stand on wooden pilings. The buildings float. The topographical contours of the land remain intact. In part they will be reconstructed, and sometimes slightly intensified. The sweep of the landscape is retained underneath the new buildings.

Building with wood is a tradition in this pre-Alpine region. New techniques of wood construction are constantly being developed and tested in Switzerland. These two facts gave us the courage to design buildings of this size completely out of wood—at once powerful and elegant.

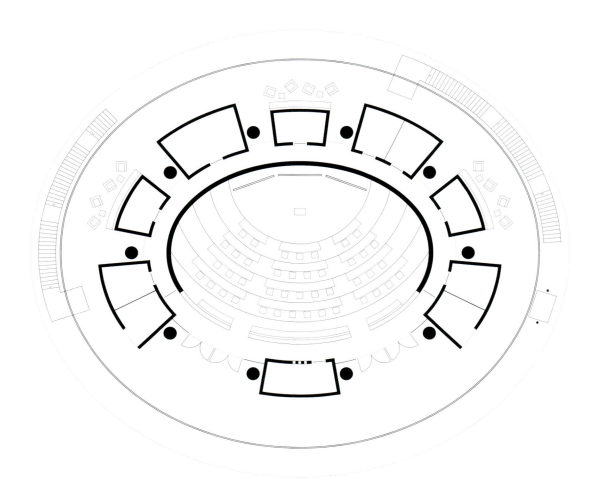

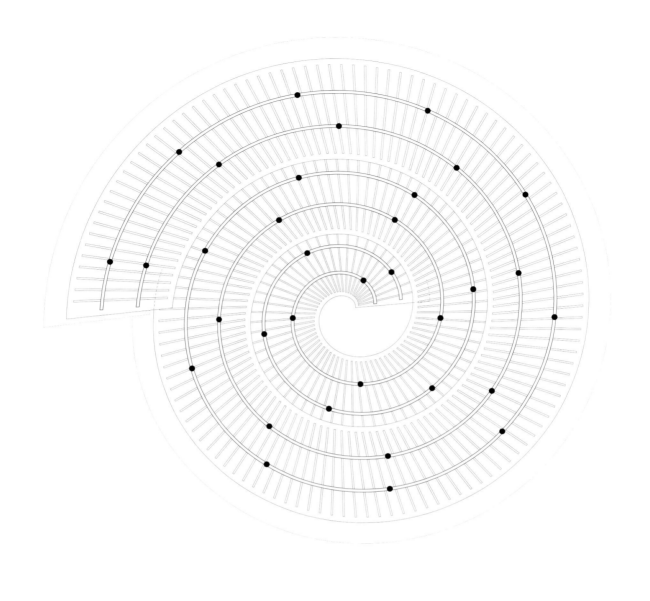
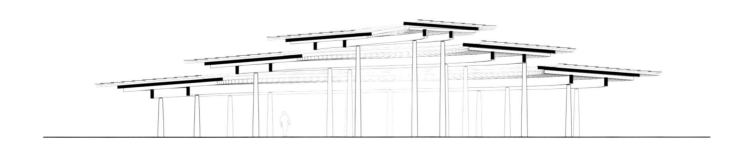

Almannajuvet Zinc Mine Museum, Sauda, Norway
since 2003

Zinc mining in the Almanna Canyon in Sauda, Norway, commenced in 1882 under extremely basic conditions. On a specially constructed trail that snaked up out of the canyon, mules dragged cartloads of ore from the mine up to the edge of the cliff, where they were hurled down to the valley floor in order to break them up into smaller pieces. There they were washed and conveyed about ten kilometers to the harbor at Sauda to be shipped to England for further processing. The mine was closed in 1899. The world market price for zinc had changed.

At about the spot where the ore used to be washed and a miners' barracks once stood on a rocky outcrop, there is now a rest stop on National Highway 520, which belongs to the Norwegian tourist highway network. These roads run a good 1800 kilometers through the country from south to north, repeatedly beckoning visitors to stop along the way at special sites to enjoy the beauty of the landscape or places of historical interest.

Our project was commissioned by the Statens vegvesen, the Norwegian Public Roads Administration, to commemorate the almost forgotten history of the zinc mine by lending the original location renewed life. On taking a closer look, one can indeed discover traces of the canyon's mining history: the transport trail beginning at the mine entrance and cut into the slope with supporting walls and bridges, the foundations of the wooden platform from which the ore was thrown down, and the remains of foundations for simple wooden structures that have since disappeared.

Our design works with these elements. It proposes a family of four structures, light wooden constructions along the old mine pathway. The modest open-air museum begins at the redesigned rest stop. Here we find the first member of the little family, a service building. Opposite the rest stop we have built a new flight of stone stairs which leads up to the former trail from the pit. A few more steps up the trail we come to the mining café. It largely serves tourists in summer but can be used for small events all year round by the residents of Sauda and environs. In the café, simple local foods and beverages are available as well as clothing and household items made by women and men from the Sauda area. We encouraged the investigation of designs on the theme of "old methods—new forms." It was important to us to involve the people of Sauda in the use and operation of the facility.

After a further turn in the canyon pathway we come upon a shelter, a collection point where those who want to take a guided tour through the mine are given a helmet with a headlamp. Right next to this, visitors climb up to the mining museum, the fourth and last member of the family of buildings, perched right on the cliff the ore used to be thrown off.

With the help of Leiv-Arild Berg, a local resident who has long been gathering information on the mine, we assembled all the documents we could find for the museum. The pickings were slim—the exhibit in our little museum shows this—but nonetheless impressive: stock certificates, purchase contracts, insurance documents, lists of hours worked, a few old photographs, and a few pieces of equipment from the mine. The work in the mine was backbreaking. Documents which prove that seem to disappear quickly, so we asked the historian Arnvid Lillehammer to write a history of the mine, and the geologist Stein-Erik Lauritzen to draw up a map and describe the mining and the geology. In addition, we commissioned Kjartan Fløgstad, the Norwegian writer who comes from Sauda, to put together an anthology of texts from world literature on the subject of being underground: *Sub Terra—Sub Sole*. The three books, each unique and designed by Aud Gloppen, are on show in the museum.

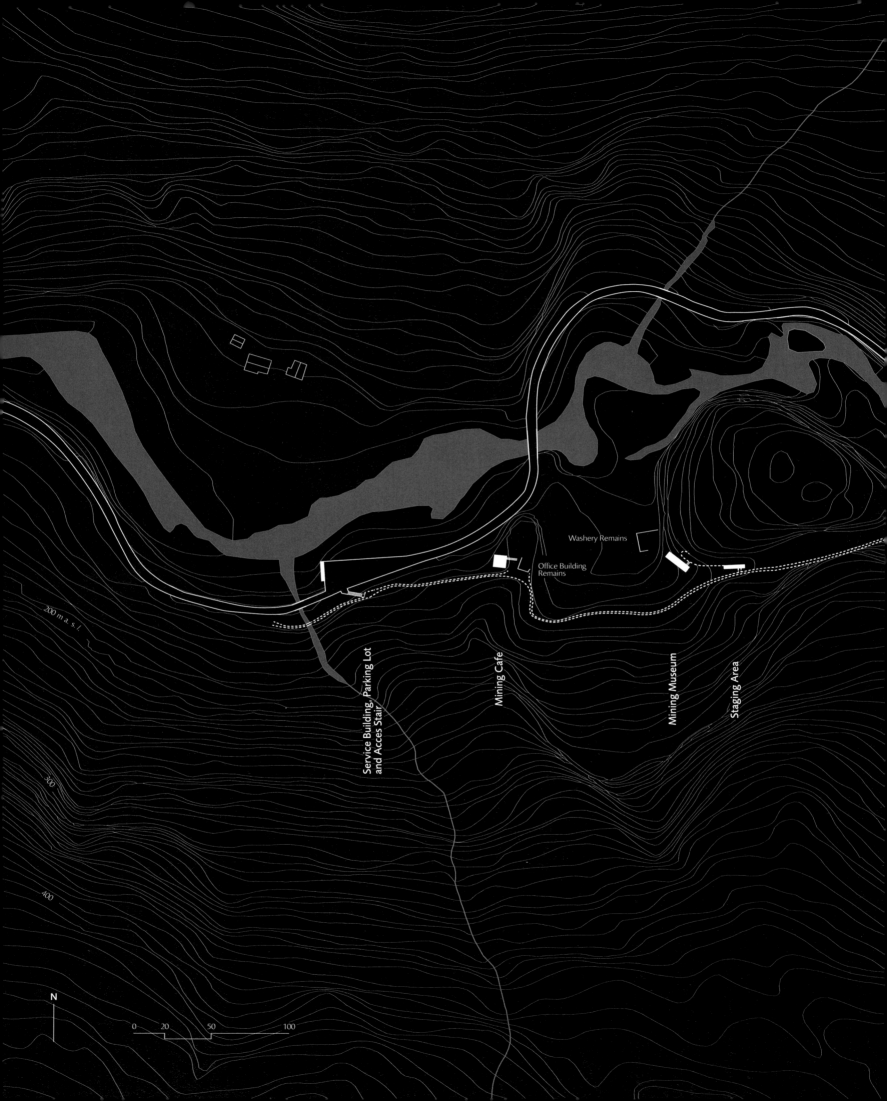

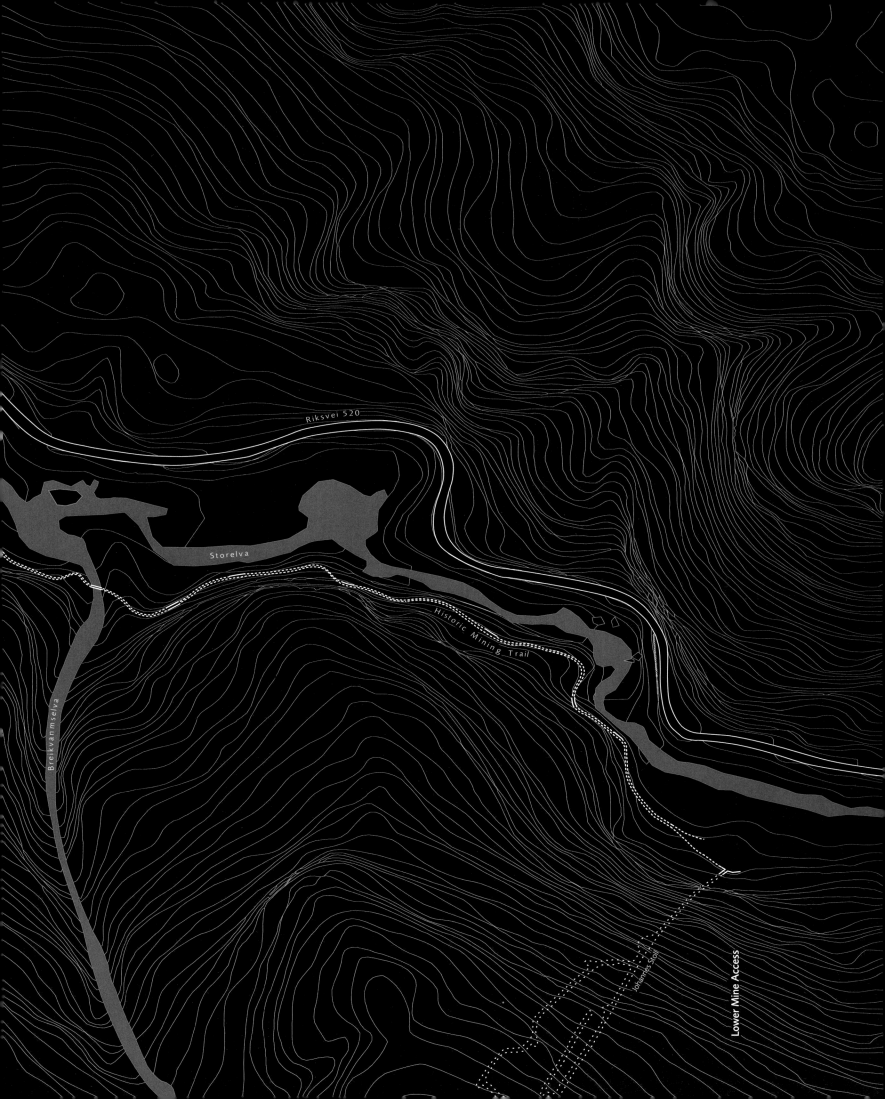

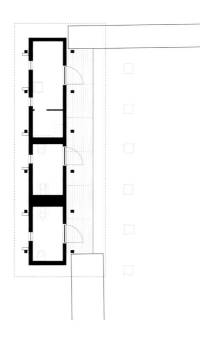
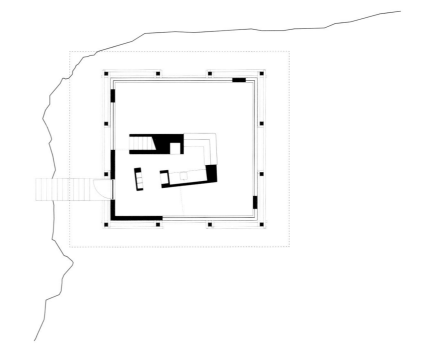
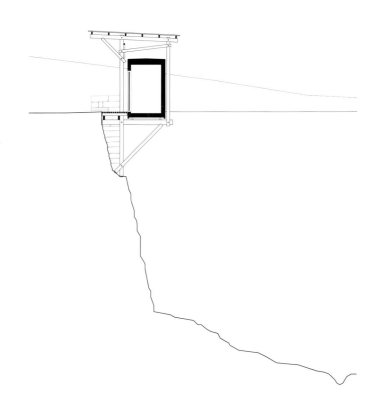
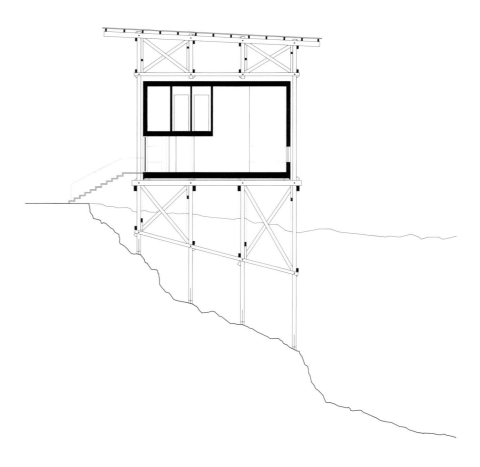

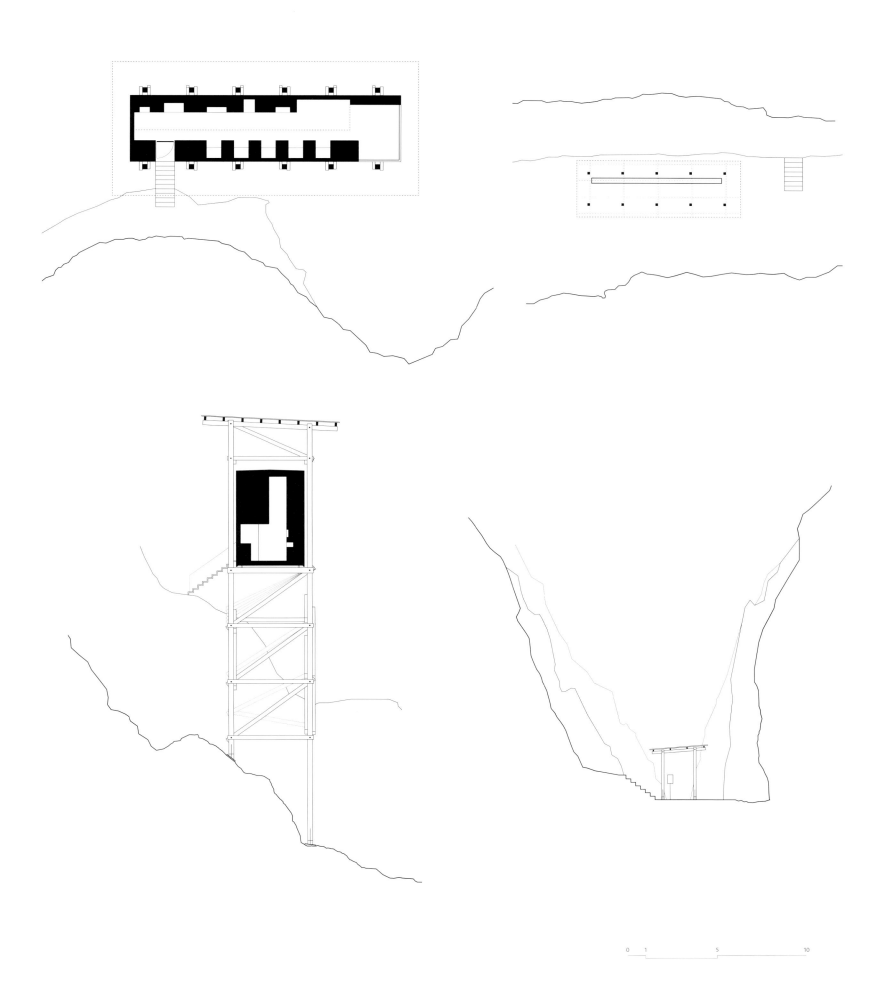

Güterareal Residential Development, Lucerne
2005 – 2006

93

Ten glass structures form an ensemble with a public character, a small energy center for the neighborhood behind the railroad station in Lucerne. Buildings and the spaces between them make for a composition based on balance, tension, and spatial density.

Actually I could easily have found out that the Swiss Federal Railways, which have for some time been capitalizing on their unused central station railyards, were not primarily interested in good architecture but in the best possible commercial exploitation of their property.

As later became evident, considerations involving a commitment to the city as a living space did not play a significant role in the process of selecting the project that would be built. But here was this well-situated piece of land in the heart of the city, this empty spot in the civic fabric, that we thought well suited to an attempt at articulating a lesson in contemporary urban living. This objective seduced us into entering the limited competition without any further advance clarifications. So we never managed to build anything, but we learned a good deal.

The site's excellent location—Old Town, station, Convention Center, and the world-famous bay of Lake Lucerne, all within comfortable walking distance—strongly suggested that we plan exclusive city apartments, for which there is a need.

The basic outline of the development works with mass and empty space. The elongated structures stand close together. The empty space between them is a continuation of the open space of the city as it flows into the ensemble and is caught up by its interlocking structures. We had studied the self-contained feeling of the Old Town across from the site, where the apartments, despite, or perhaps because of, the density of the buildings, enjoy great popularity; I remembered my daughter Anna Katharina saying to me that she would prefer a specially tailored apartment or even one with just a single, remarkably shaped room to a standard apartment any time. And so we tailored the apartments individually, in glass buildings that relate with urbane elegance to the shared free space, scaled to match the Old Town.

In the course of the design work we discovered the advantage of buildings facing each other. Unlike living next to or above other dwellings, the idea we proposed of living opposite one another creates a special sense of community, generated by the combination of spatial proximity and the feeling of sheltered autonomy—a fruitful contrast of nearness and distance, a stimulation of neighborly feelings.

hauptskizze 1:500 nov. 05
Ortsgebiet Stk Ivan
Wettbewerb

Wohnungsmix:

35x12=420m² 35x12=600m²   8x30=240m²

(Front how) haus

3-4 Hohe
30x12=360m²

35x12= 10x15= 55x15=825m²
24x12=   150m²
              38x11=418m²

Reihen 8-12 Individuell
+ Physiotherm

Atrius, Reihhauser, Bung...

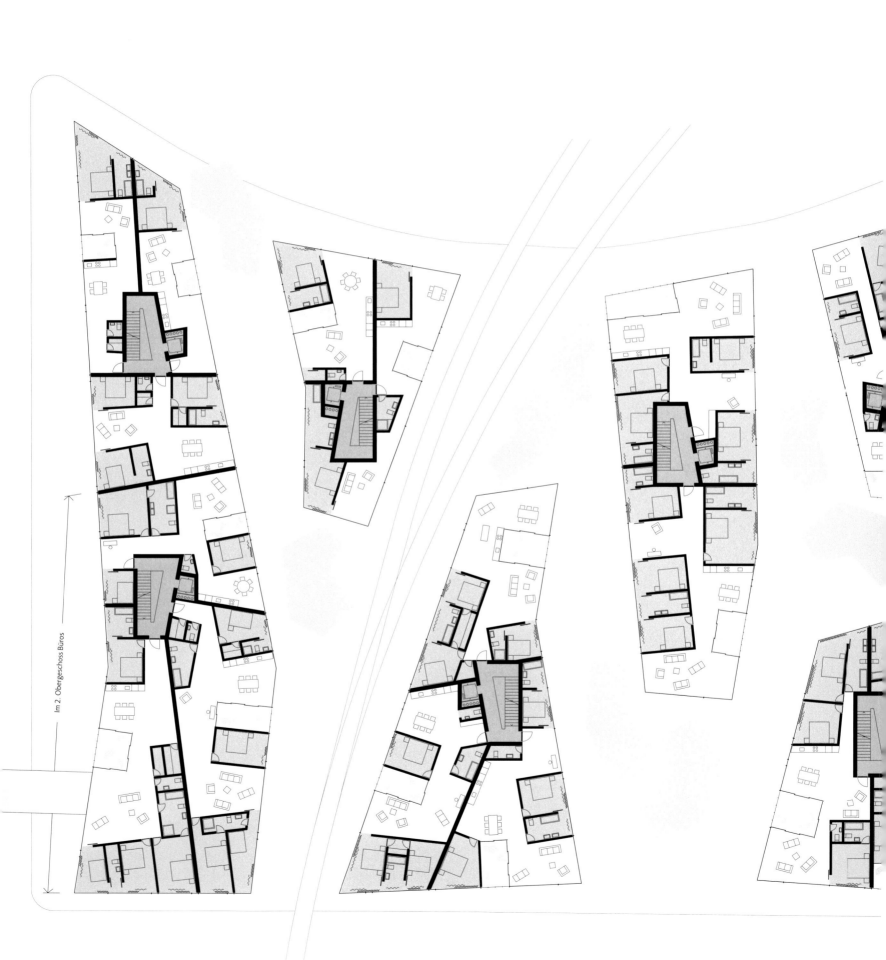

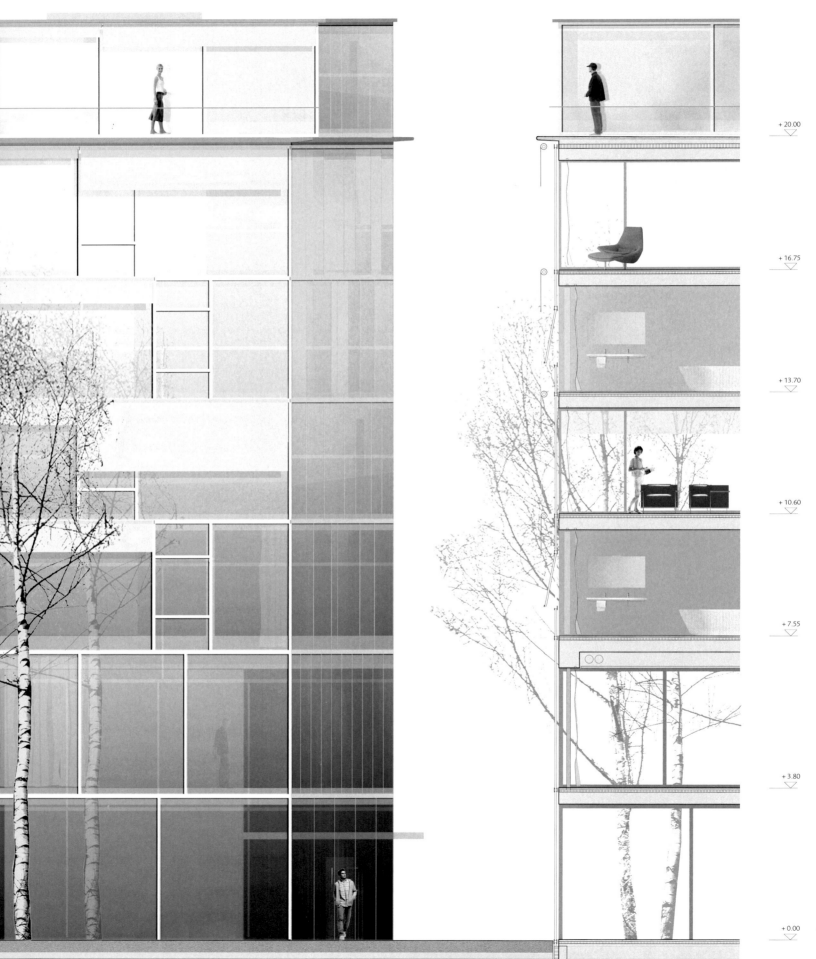

A Tower for Therme Vals, Graubünden
2005 – 2012

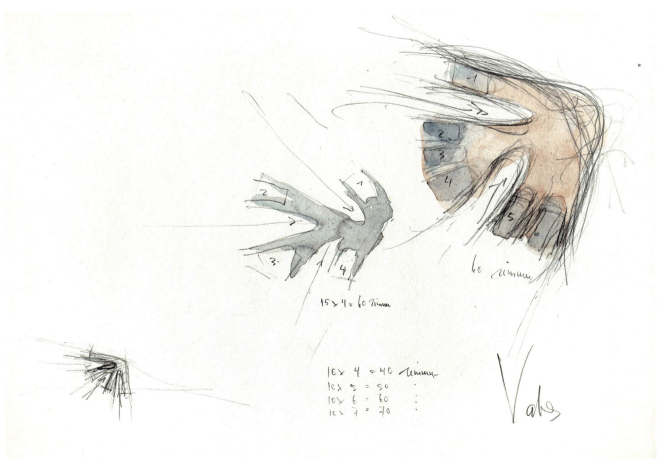

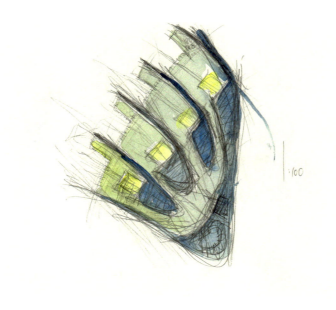

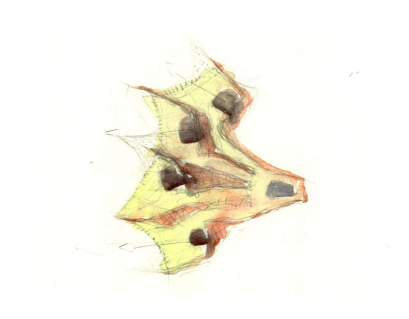

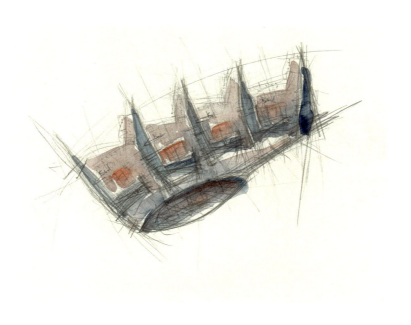

I love hotels, these short-term living communities. The tension between the intimate privacy of the rooms and the semi-anonymous public life of the lobby, bar, and restaurant creates a special atmosphere that fascinates me.

In Vals I designed a little bedroom tower for the woods above the spa, an atmospheric sketch for the hotel of my dreams, which I still have not built. The tower, its walls dividing and unfolding as it rises out of the evergreen forest, is a celebration of the view and the landscape. Leaving the access corridor to the rear and standing at one of the viewing bays fanning out from inside the rooms, you practically float in the sky—the feeling is freedom.

Leis Houses, Oberhus and Unterhus, Vals, Graubünden
2006–2009

I first came across the wooden farmhouses of Graubünden in the seventies.
While working as an architect for the regional historic preservation authority,
I had studied their construction and typological evolution over the centuries,
and I assumed this kind of construction was on its way to extinction. But then
my wife Annalisa, who dreamed of living in a wooden house someday,
and Valentin and Lillian Luzi in Jenaz, who asked me to design a wooden house
for them, made me wonder whether I could do something new with wooden
beams. I began to rethink building with solid wood from the point of view of
material and construction, and this soon freed my imagination. Memories
of all the stuffiness and dust when I had inventoried and renovated these old
houses years before evaporated. I saw the possibility of doing construction
with shear walls, opposing surfaces, of making rooms as if playing with a house
of cards. What resulted from the design phase reminded me of the buildings
of the De Stijl architects of the twenties in Holland, who worked with similar
principles in creating spaces.
In my piece on the Luzi House in Jenaz, I described the problems we had
to solve and the answers we came up with.
The Leis Houses—the Oberhus, the Unterhus, and the Türmlihus that completes the little group—stand at the end of this small research project
on the theme of building with solid wood beams. While the construction of the
Luzi House (2002) in principle consists of five wooden towers and four
intermediary spaces, the Oberhus is made of load-bearing cells—rectangular
wooden boxes characteristic of the method we developed for massive
beam construction—stacked on top of one another, their shape and layout
varying from floor to floor. The physical and spatial joins are complex.
Portions of the rooms are cantilevered outward making large bays or oriels.
The outer ends of projecting shear walls are tensioned to each other with
steel cables.
The living and sleeping areas are located in the bays projecting from the façade.
These bays have generously sized glass windows. The mountain landscape
scenes, changing with the seasons, time of day, and weather, come right into the
house. You can sit snugly in a bay window, as if in a box at the theater,
and experience nature at first hand: storms, snow, wind, fog, ominous skies,
and radiant light streaming on the land.

Traditionally, carpenters cut and tailor their timber to size in the workshop and then assemble the construction on site. Contemporary drawing and manufacturing techniques represent another stage in this tradition of prefabrication. We needed over five thousand separate beams for the walls, ceilings, and roofs of the Oberhus and the Unterhus, which were built at the same time. At the lumber factory, a computerized framing machine cut them to the proper size with all the required notches, ridges, beads, bore holes, and gaps. The windows, doors, and utility installations could then be inserted on site, without any further treatment of the wood itself.

All the planning data from our shop drawings was digitized and entered into the lumber factory's computer and, after necessary adjustments, fed into the framing machine, which produced all the tailored pieces of lumber.

After that, the work proceeded as it did a thousand years ago. This was in three beautiful weeks in the late summer of 2008 in Leis. The carpenters stood out in the open air on the ever taller walls, piling tier upon tier of wooden beams. The rhythmic beat of the sledgehammers resounded brightly, the fresh wood smelled good, and it was a joy to watch the rooms grow.

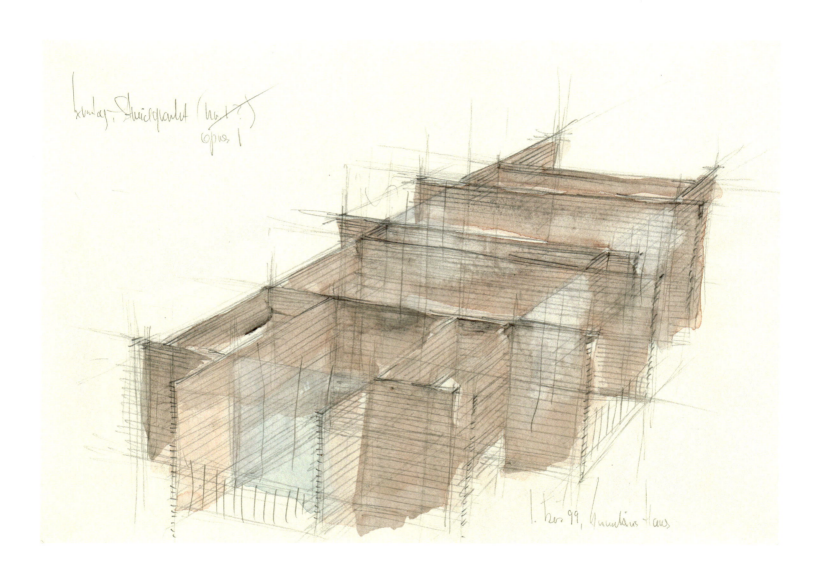

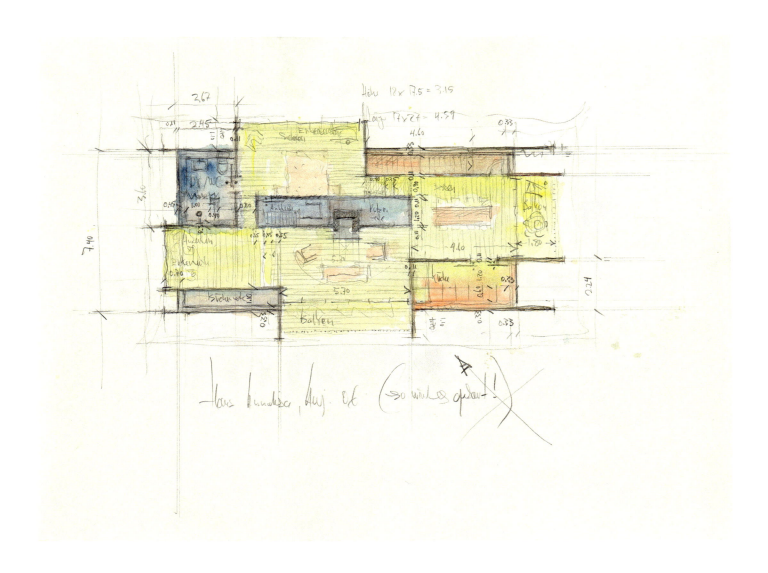

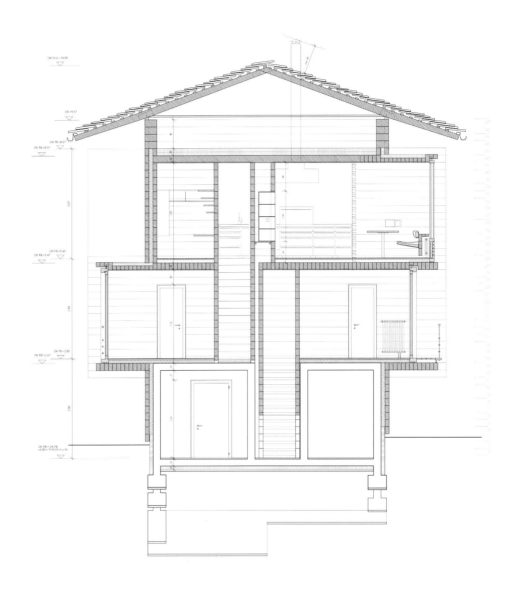

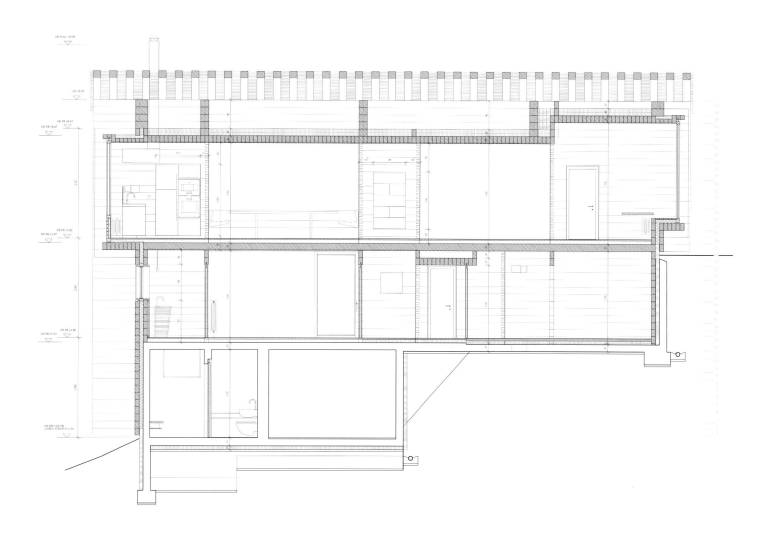

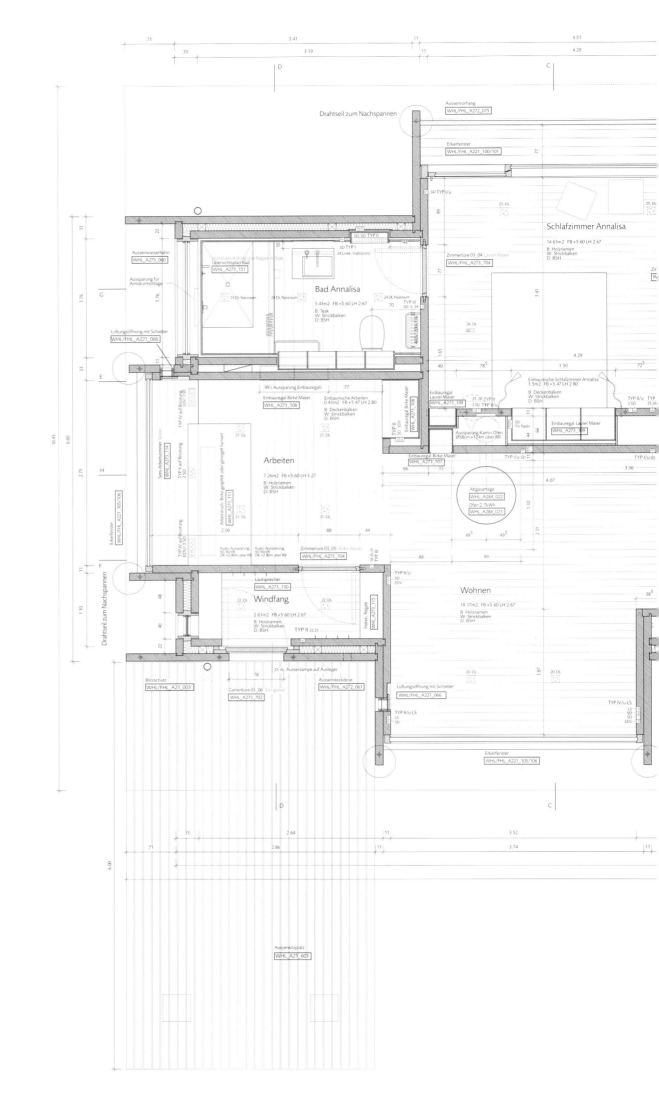

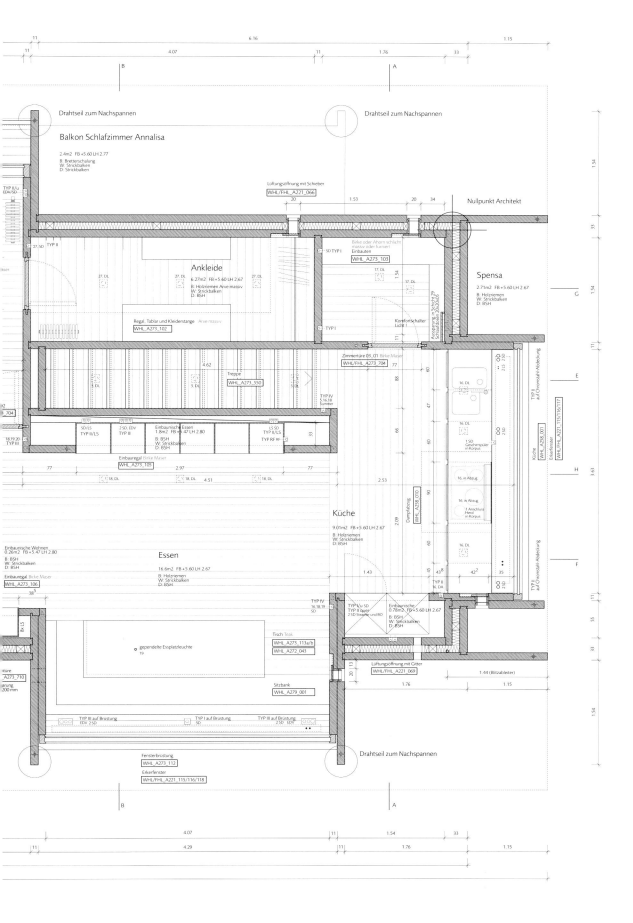

Hisham's Palace, House of Mosaics, Jericho,
Palestinian Territories
2006–2010

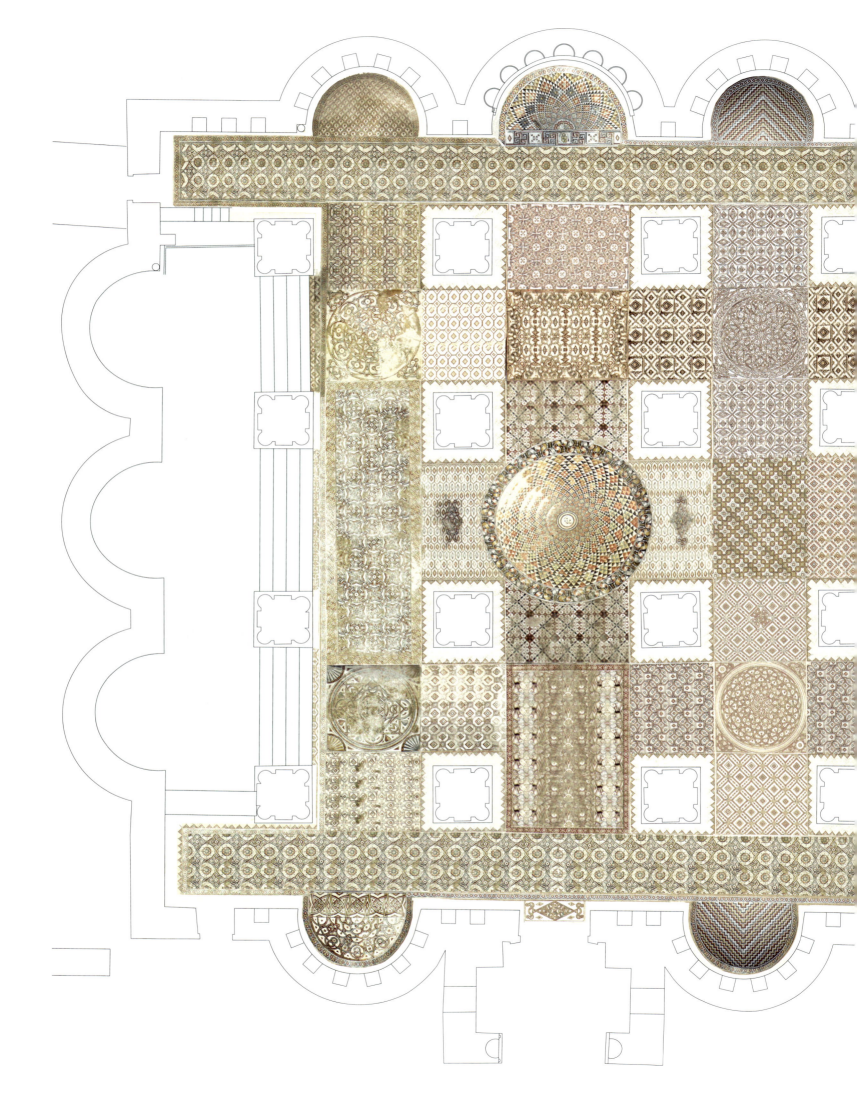

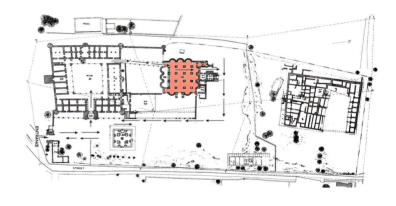

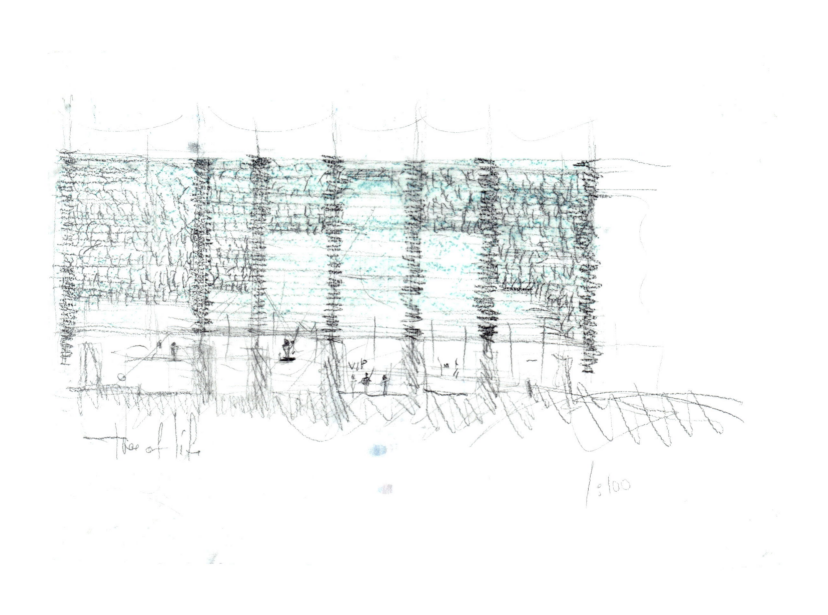

Built during the Umayyad dynasty, Hisham's Palace is considered one of the earliest examples of Islamic architecture. The winter palace, named after Caliph Hisham bin Abed el-Malik (691–743), was built by his successor el-Walid II from 733 to 734. Except for the great bath house—as I learned from historical descriptions—the grand residence in the Jordan Valley, at 260 meters below sea level, was never completed. The bath house, according to these reports, was destroyed by an earthquake in 749. But the extraordinarily valuable mosaic floor of the bath house was preserved beneath the rubble. It was excavated in the 1930s and 40s and later documented by the British archaeologist Robert W. Hamilton. Today a protective layer of sand covers the mosaics, so they cannot be seen.

To understand and get a sense of the spatial experience the bath house originally imparted, we built a ten-to-one scale model of it on the site, based on Hamilton's drawings and with the help of local architects, engineers, and employees of the museum. The model stands on supports so that the inside is visible through a hole in the floor plate. When I looked into the model through this hole, I saw an interior of sacral appearance, the original of which must have cast a soft muted light over the mosaics on the floor. This experience informed our design work. It was not the first time I had felt the desire to bring back to life some of the original atmosphere of a lost building by placing a protective shell over its remains.

With a commission from Unesco we designed a light, floating volume made of cedar that covers and protects the ruins of the bath house. The hollow space inside contains an abstract reconstruction of the bath house that was destroyed by the earthquake. Beams laid crosswise over each other form a large support grid, whose footprint duplicates the spatial structure of the lost building. In the coffers of this grid there is a meshwork ceiling formed of black staves interwoven in crisscross fashion reminiscent of the traditional *mashrabiya* technique. The height of the meshwork varies to represent the different ceiling heights of the original interior: low in the side aisles and high in the central aisle.

The floating protective structure has hollow ceiling spaces visible from below and rests on masonry pilasters deriving from an earlier, supposedly Jordanian reconstruction effort in the sixties of the last century.

We have installed a system of simple catwalks in the new wooden structure. Under the shelter of the large roof overhead, visitors climb up to the circular walkway from outside. There they can see the floor mosaics, now clear of sand, from above, including the famous Tree of Life in the Divan, the caliph's reception room, which adjoins the main room.

For the palace area as a whole, we worked up a master plan with two irrigated gardens, a vegetable garden, *bustan*, and a flower garden, *hadiqa*. We wanted to bring back to life some of the original atmosphere of the palace. This structure, shimmering in the sun, was conceived for the protection and better understanding of the extant ruins of the bath house here on the embattled plain of the Jordan Valley, the West Bank. It could become a landmark of indigenous culture, one that is visible far and wide. The thought pleases us.

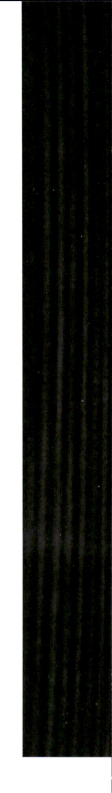

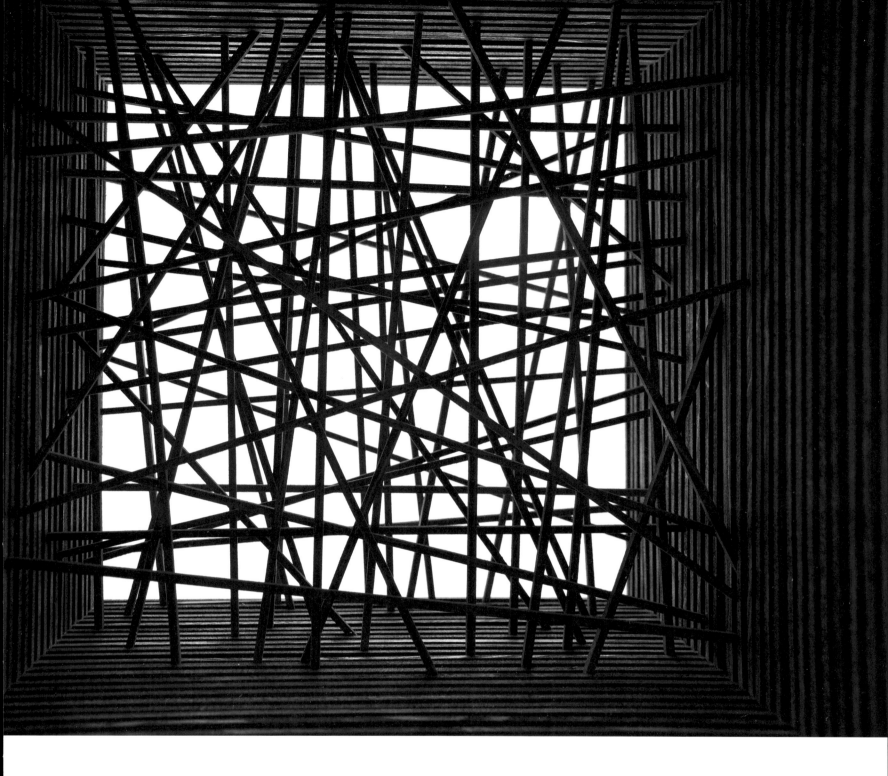

Steilneset, Memorial to the Victims of the Witch Trials
in the Finnmark, Vardø, Norway
2007–2011

167

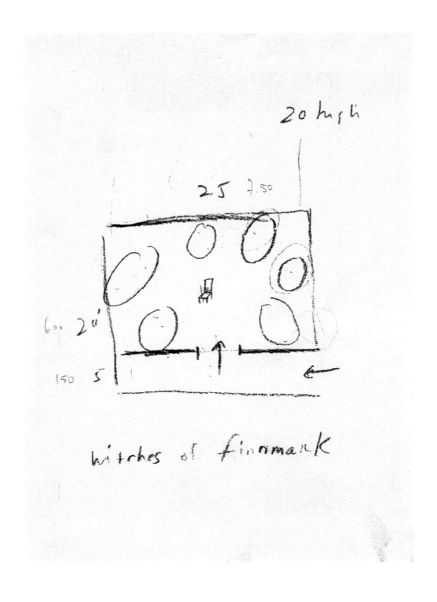

Vardø is a small island off the Norwegian mainland in the Barents Sea north of the Arctic Circle. The treeless landscape of this region is impressive. The scrubby vegetation on the rocky soil seems to be cowering in the wind. At first glance it is nothing much to look at, but on closer examination, it reveals a delicate carpet of plants in a diversity of exquisite forms, gleaming with the intense colors of small flowers.

Vardø was once an attractive fishing village. Today there are only a few boats left in the inner harbor, and the long wooden racks in the landscape, once used to dry fish, are falling apart. Many of the houses are empty. There are now hardly any living-room windows at which, by ancient custom, a lamp is lit at nightfall. I noticed this on my arrival in the winter of 2007, traveling in planes that had gotten smaller and smaller with each successive airfield.

From 1600 to 1692, ninety-one people in Vardø were condemned as witches and burned; most were women, but some were men, from the indigenous Sami (formerly called Lapp) population. Before being bound to a stake and burned, they were tried in court proceedings. The trial documents have been preserved. Historian Liv Helene Willumsen published them with commentaries in her book *The Witchcraft Trials in Finnmark Northern Norway* (Leikanger, 2010).

Based on these documents, Willumsen wrote short biographical texts for our project on each of those burned as witches. We inscribed her texts on ninety-one silk cloths and hung them inside the new building that now, after so long, will finally commemorate the murdered victims. Beside each cloth hanging there, on which we can read the absurd actions to which the victims confessed after a few days' trial, there is a small window with a light inside that is always burning.

Our building is a floating passageway of fabric. It is made of fiberglass canvas coated with Teflon, which looks rather like sailcloth. The flexible textile form is stretched on a wooden frame and is big enough to contain the ninety-one windows and texts. It moves with the constant coastal wind. The light bulbs suspended in front of the windows sway gently.

Steilneset is the name of the seaside location where the elongated building stands, and it is the actual spot where the sentenced victims were burned at the stake. The burning itself is memorialized in an installation by Louise Bourgeois, for which we built an enclosure, made of seventeen free-standing glass panels. She faxed us a sketch of her specifications; it is reproduced on page 170. The installation within the pavilion consists of seven large mirrors reflecting multiple and distorted images of a fire blazing up from the seat of a chair.

Liv Helene Willumsen's texts on the silk cloths inside the long building are succinct linguistic works of art. Under the name of each victim stands the date of birth, the date of burning, the charges, the victim's confession, and, finally, the verdict, almost always the same: to be burned at the stake. When we walk through the building and become engaged with the texts, we learn something important about lives long past, about injustice masquerading as law, and about death.

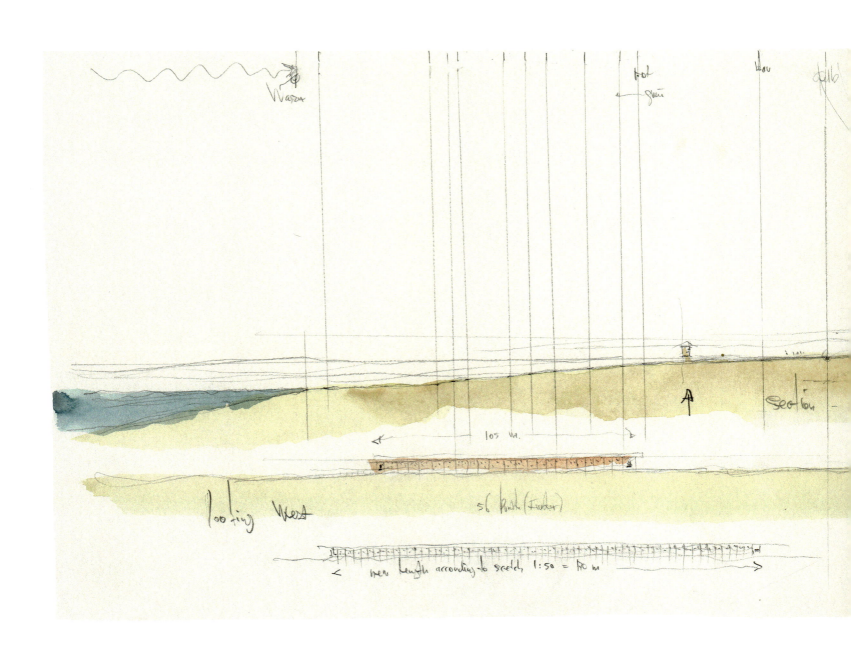

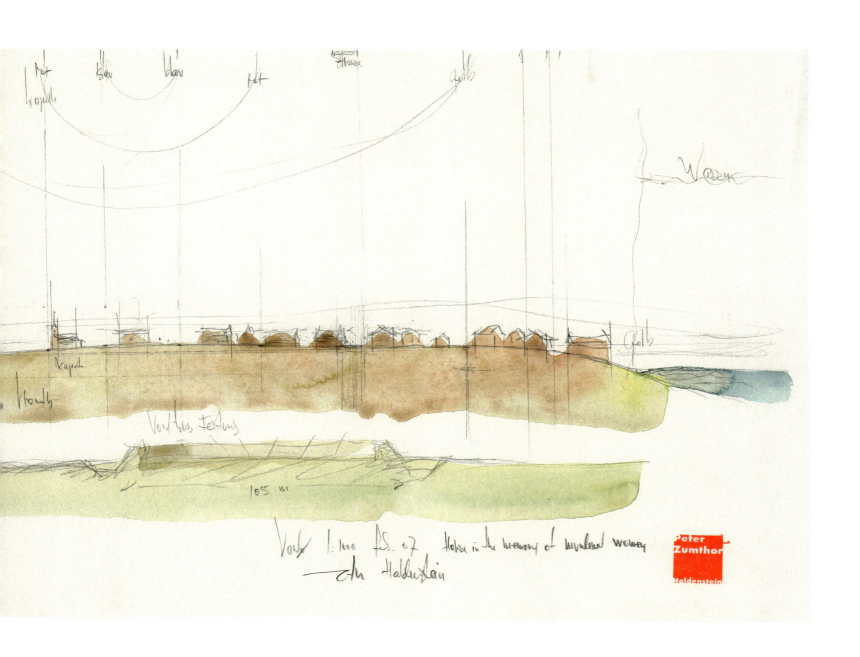

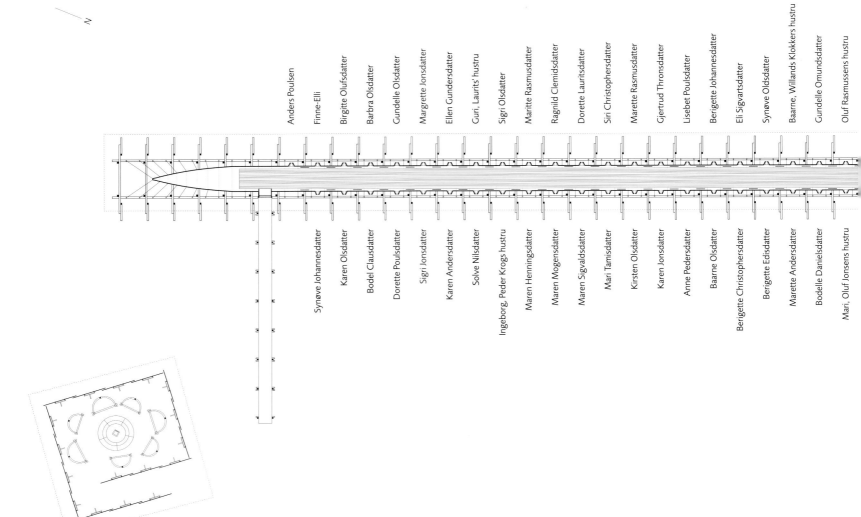

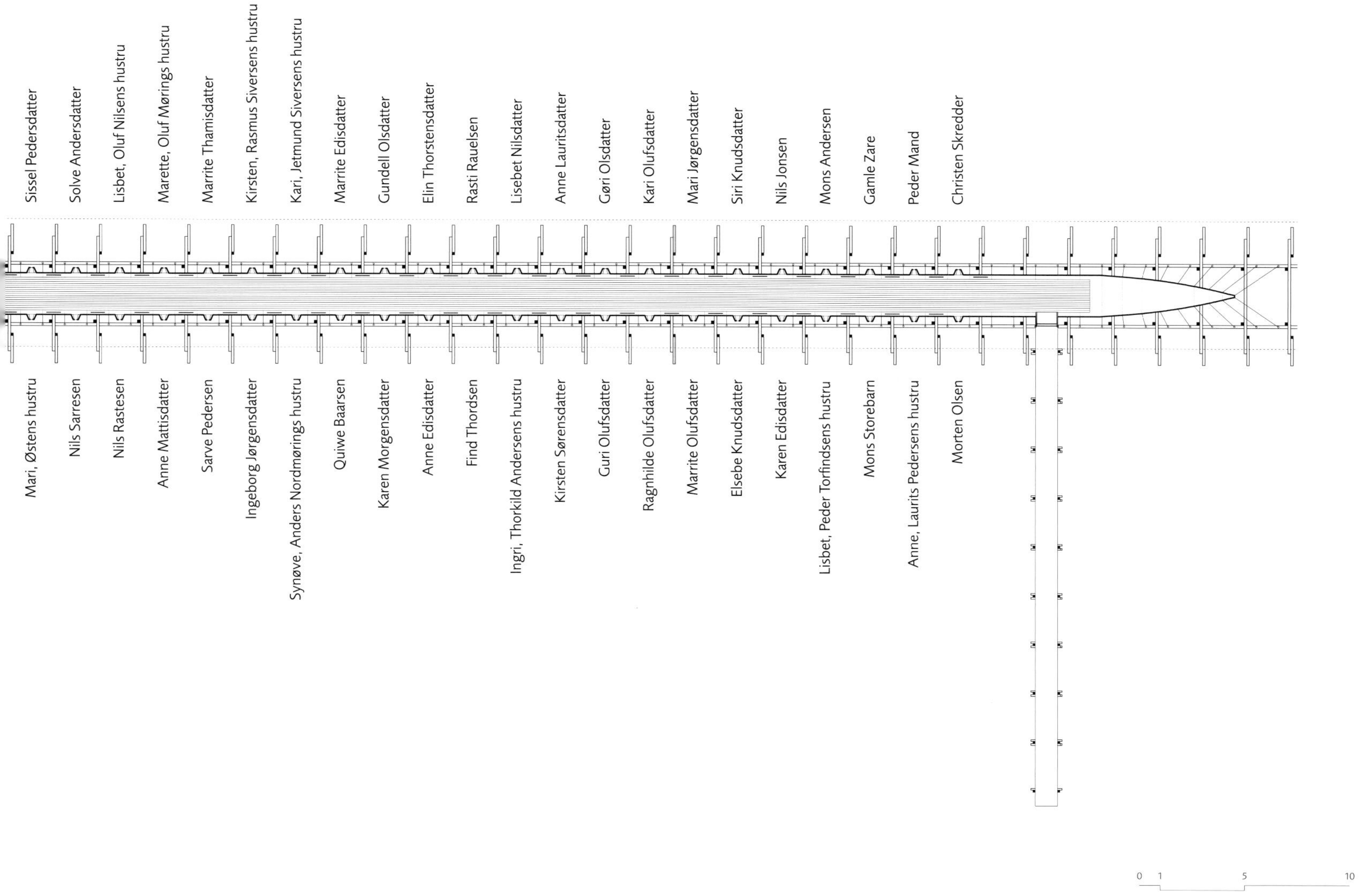
Sissel Pedersdatter
Solve Andersdatter
Lisbet, Oluf Nilsens hustru
Marette, Oluf Mørings hustru
Marrite Thamisdatter
Kirsten, Rasmus Siversens hustru
Kari, Jetmund Siversens hustru
Marrite Edisdatter
Gundell Olsdatter
Elin Thorstensdatter
Rasti Rauelsen
Lisebet Nilsdatter
Anne Lauritsdatter
Gøri Olsdatter
Kari Olufsdatter
Mari Jørgensdatter
Siri Knudsdatter
Nils Jonsen
Mons Andersen
Gamle Zare
Peder Mand
Christen Skredder
Mari, Østens hustru
Nils Sarresen
Nils Rastesen
Anne Mattisdatter
Sarve Pedersen
Ingeborg Jørgensdatter
Synøve, Anders Nordmørings hustru
Quiwe Baarsen
Karen Morgensdatter
Anne Edisdatter
Find Thordsen
Ingri, Thorkild Andersens hustru
Kirsten Sørensdatter
Guri Olufsdatter
Ragnhilde Olufsdatter
Marrite Olufsdatter
Elsebe Knudsdatter
Karen Edisdatter
Lisbet, Peder Torfindsens hustru
Mons Storebarn
Anne, Laurits Pedersens hustru
Morten Olsen
0 1 5 10

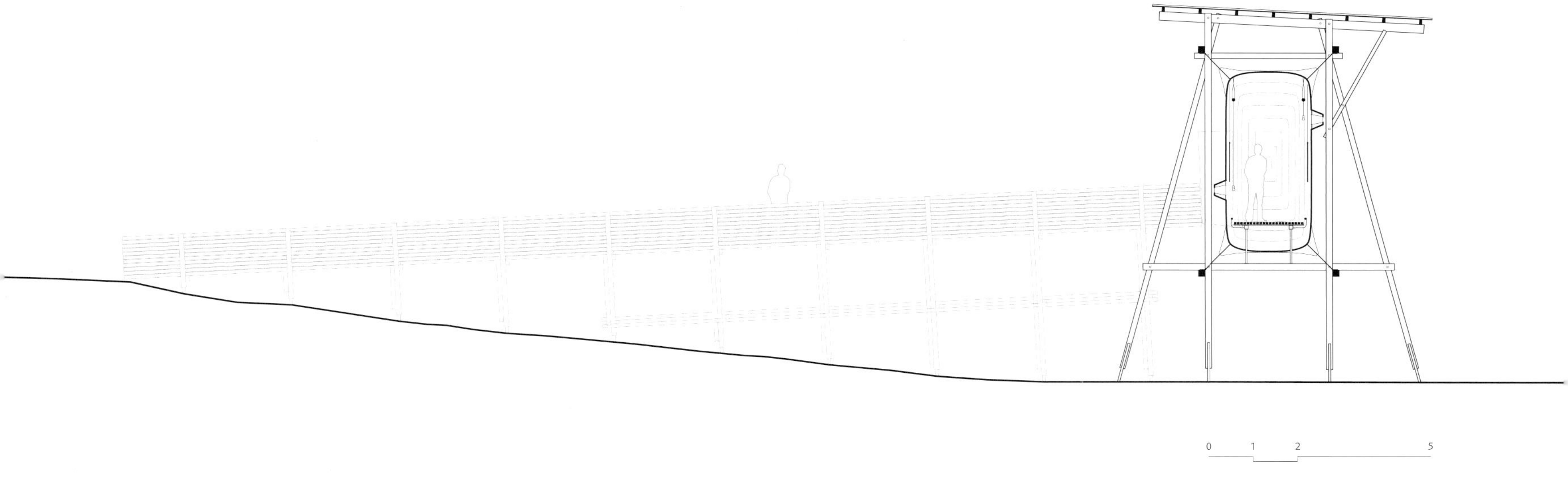
0 1 2 5

Concept: Peter Zumthor, Thomas Durisch, Beat Keusch
Design: Beat Keusch Visuelle Kommunikation, Basel – Beat Keusch, Angelina Köpplin
Artistic advice: Arpaïs Du Bois
Translation: John Hargraves
Editing: Catherine Schelbert
Proofreading: Bronwen Saunders
Image processing: Georg Sidler, Samuel Trutmann
Printing and binding: DZA Druckerei zu Altenburg GmbH, Thüringen

Picture credits, see appendix, volume 5

This book is volume 4 of *Peter Zumthor 1985–2013,* a set of five volumes which are not available separately.

© 2014 Verlag Scheidegger & Spiess AG, Zurich

New edition 2024: ISBN 978-3-03942-248-7

German edition: ISBN 978-3-03942-247-0

Verlag Scheidegger & Spiess AG
Niederdorfstrasse 54
8001 Zurich
Switzerland

Scheidegger & Spiess is being supported by the Federal Office of Culture with a general subsidy for the years 2021–2024.

All rights reserved; no part of this publication may be reproduced, stored in a retrieval system or transmitted in any form or by any means, electronic, mechanical, photocopying, recording or otherwise, without the prior written consent of the publisher.

www.scheidegger-spiess.ch